MILITARY SHIPS
AIRCRAFT CARRIERS

BY JOHN HAMILTON

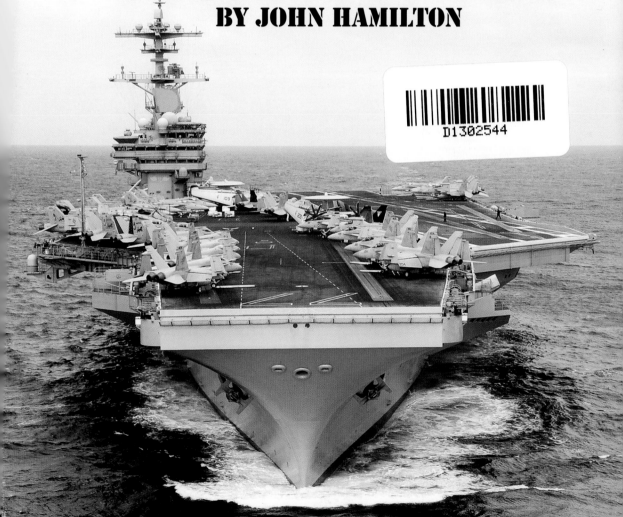

VISIT US AT
WWW.ABDOPUBLISHING.COM

Published by ABDO Publishing Company, PO Box 398166, Minneapolis, MN 55439.
Copyright ©2013 by Abdo Consulting Group, Inc. International copyrights reserved in all
countries. No part of this book may be reproduced in any form without written permission
from the publisher. A&D Xtreme™ is a trademark and logo of ABDO Publishing Company.

Printed in the United States of America, North Mankato, Minnesota.
032012
092012

Editor: Sue Hamilton
Graphic Design: Sue Hamilton
Cover Design: John Hamilton
Cover Photo: United States Navy
Interior Photos: All photos United States Navy except AP-pg 29 (graphic); Department of
Defense-pgs 10-11; Naval Historical Center-pg 8; Newport News Shipbuilding-pgs 16, 17
& 18-19.

ABDO Booklinks
Web sites about Military Ships are featured on our Book Links pages. These links are
routinely monitored and updated to provide the most current information available.
Web site: www.abdopublishing.com

Library of Congress Cataloging-in-Publication Data

Hamilton, John, 1959-
   Aircraft carriers / John Hamilton.
       p. cm. -- (Military ships)
   Includes index.
   ISBN 978-1-61783-519-3
   1. Aircraft carriers--Juvenile literature. I. Title.
   V874.H357 2012
   623.825'5--dc23
                        2012005056

TABLE OF CONTENTS

AIRCRAFT CARRIERS

Aircraft carriers are the largest ships in the United States Navy's fleet. The Navy uses these powerful ships all over the world to launch airplanes and helicopters.

Because of aircraft carriers, the United States does not need to rely as much on air bases in other countries. Aircraft carriers can project U.S. military might almost anywhere in the world. Their presence prevents potential enemies from attacking the U.S. and its allies.

USS John C. Stennis receiving supplies while underway.

XTREME FACT

The United States currently has 11 aircraft carriers, more than any other country in the world.

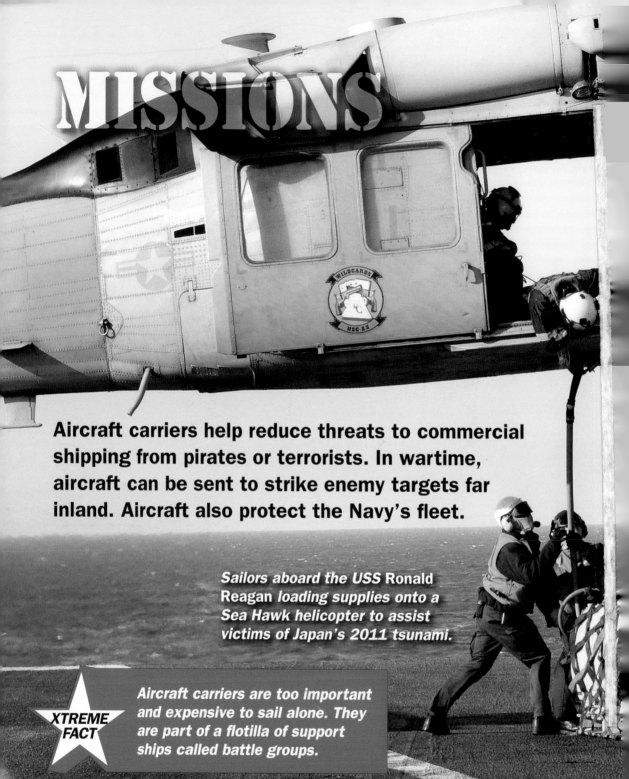

MISSIONS

Aircraft carriers help reduce threats to commercial shipping from pirates or terrorists. In wartime, aircraft can be sent to strike enemy targets far inland. Aircraft also protect the Navy's fleet.

Sailors aboard the USS Ronald Reagan loading supplies onto a Sea Hawk helicopter to assist victims of Japan's 2011 tsunami.

XTREME FACT

Aircraft carriers are too important and expensive to sail alone. They are part of a flotilla of support ships called battle groups.

Aircraft carriers are also used on disaster-relief missions. This includes airlifting supplies to earthquake or tsunami victims.

HISTORY

A crane loading the biplane onto the ship.

The first airplane took off from a warship in November 1910. Eugene Ely piloted a Curtiss Model D biplane launched from the deck of the USS *Birmingham*. At first, ship-launched airplanes were used as scouts.

Eugene Ely piloting his Curtiss Model D biplane from the deck of the USS Birmingham on November 14, 1910. The flight lasted for about five minutes.

During World War II, American and Japanese navies in the Pacific Ocean used aircraft carriers to attack enemy ships and targets inland.

An American plane flying over an aircraft carrier in the Pacific Ocean in 1943.

TYPES OF AIRCRAFT CARRIERS

The 11 capital ships of the United States Navy are called supercarriers. These nuclear-powered vessels are the largest warships in the world. Many navies rely on medium and light aircraft carriers. These are smaller vessels with fewer planes. Amphibious assault ships are also small aircraft carriers. They use helicopters or jets that can take off and land vertically.

An F/A-18 Super Hornet taking off from the deck of the USS Enterprise, *the only Enterprise-class supercarrier still in service.*

XTREME FACT

Ten U.S. supercarriers are Nimitz-class ships. They are longer than three football fields, measuring 1,092 feet (333 m).

Amphibious assault ship USS Guam

Supercarrier USS John F. Kennedy

British aircraft carrier
HMS Ark Royal

AIRCRAFT CARRIER FAST FACTS

Nimitz-Class Supercarriers Specifications

Length:	1,092 feet (333 m)
Width (beam):	134 feet (41 m)
Displacement:	97,000 tons (87,997 metric tons)
Propulsion:	Two nuclear reactors, four shafts
Speed:	30-plus knots (35 mph/56 kph)
Crew:	3,000-3,200 — Ship's Company
	1,500 — Air Wing
	500 — Other
Aircraft:	60-85
Cost:	About $4.5 billion each

An artistic image of the new Gerald R. Ford-class aircraft carrier.

The USS Gerald R. Ford *is a new-generation aircraft carrier. It is scheduled to enter service in 2015. These new Ford-class ships will use more automation and advanced electronics, plus a new nuclear reactor design.*

XTREME FACT

Nimitz-class aircraft carriers are designed with a 50-year service lifespan, which includes one refueling overhaul of the nuclear reactor.

CREW

America's supercarriers have between 5,000 and 6,000 people aboard. They are like floating cities. They have their own hospitals, barbershops, athletic facilities, and chapels. They even have their own ZIP codes.

Sailors playing basketball on the USS *Nimitz.*

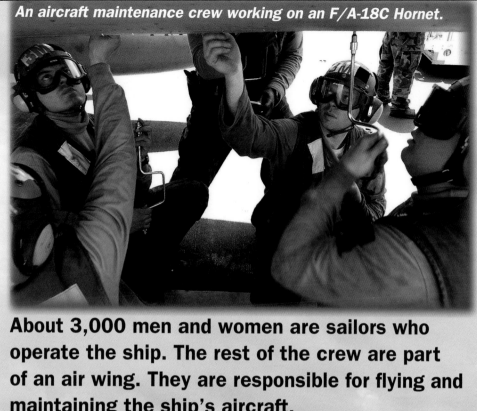

An aircraft maintenance crew working on an F/A-18C Hornet.

About 3,000 men and women are sailors who operate the ship. The rest of the crew are part of an air wing. They are responsible for flying and maintaining the ship's aircraft.

XTREME FACT

An aircraft carrier's galleys and mess halls serve between 15,000 to 18,000 meals per day.

CONSTRUCTION

Aircraft carriers are built at the Newport News Shipbuilding shipyard in Virginia. It takes several years to build a ship. They are constructed in special dry docks. The hull is made of thick steel plates.

The USS George H.W. Bush under construction in 2006.

Carriers are assembled in sections called superlifts. They contain many rooms. Superlifts can weigh as much as 900 tons (816 metric tons). Once completed, huge cranes carefully lift them into position. Then they are welded in place.

The island structure of the aircraft carrier USS Ronald Reagan is lifted into place in November 2000.

NEWPORT NEWS SHIPBUILDING

76

PROPULSION

Supercarriers get their power from two nuclear reactors. The heat from the reactors creates high-pressure steam. This steam drives the ship's propellers, as well as other ship systems. The reactors also provide electricity.

XTREME FACT

The ship's reactors are heavily shielded and closely watched to prevent a nuclear disaster.

Aircraft carriers are driven through the water by four huge propellers. Each propeller weighs about 66,200 pounds (30,028 kg). Shown here are two of the propellers for the USS George H.W. Bush, installed in 2006.

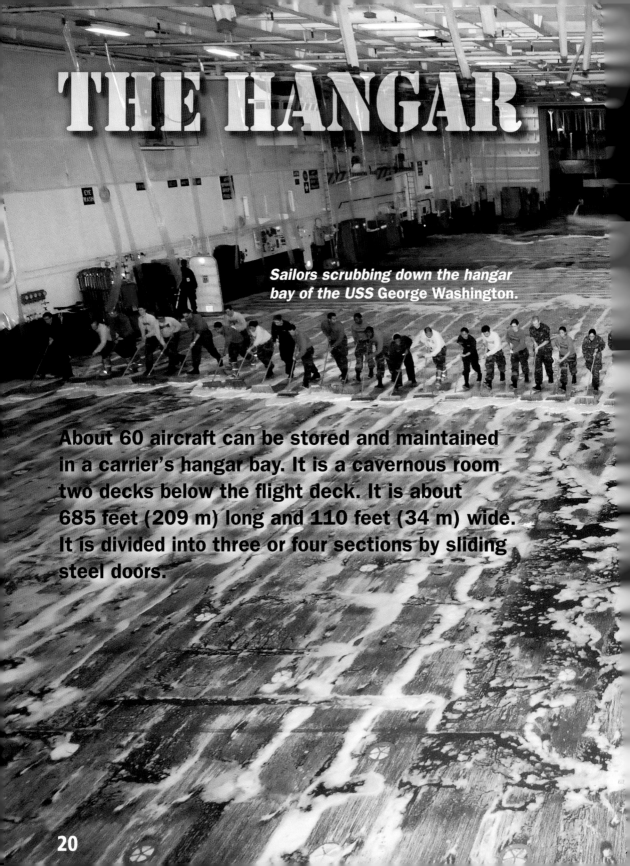

THE HANGAR

Sailors scrubbing down the hangar bay of the USS George Washington.

About 60 aircraft can be stored and maintained in a carrier's hangar bay. It is a cavernous room two decks below the flight deck. It is about 685 feet (209 m) long and 110 feet (34 m) wide. It is divided into three or four sections by sliding steel doors.

Four huge elevators lift aircraft to and from the hangar. These hydraulically powered elevators are strong enough to lift two aircraft at once.

FLIGHT DECK

The flight deck is the flat, upper part of the ship where aircraft take off and land. It is a loud and dangerous place.

XTREME FACT

When everything is working smoothly, an aircraft carrier can launch or land a plane about every 25 seconds.

Crew members wear different colored jerseys so they can be easily recognized. For example, people who handle weapons wear red jerseys. People responsible for launching planes are called shooters. They wear yellow jerseys.

THE ISLAND

The island is a narrow tower on the flight deck. It is about 150 feet (46 m) tall. On top are radar and communications antennas. They help keep track of nearby ships and planes.

The top deck of the island is the Primary Flight Control, or Pri-Fly. Underneath the Pri-Fly is the bridge. From here, the captain, a helmsman, and other officers direct the ship's movements. Other decks on the island

An air officer, or "air boss," directs aircraft takeoffs and landings.

include areas for controlling flight operations and aircraft handling.

An F/A-18 Super Hornet in front of the island of the USS Enterprise.

BEWARE OF JET BLAST PROPS

104

TAKING OFF

U.S. Navy pilots fly several types of aircraft. These include F/A-18 Hornets and Super Hornets. In the near future, advanced F-35 Lightning II fighters will also be flown.

An F/A-18 Super Hornet catapults from the aircraft carrier USS Ronald Reagan.

Flight decks are much shorter than land-based runways. Four steam-powered catapults generate the speed needed for aircraft to become airborne.

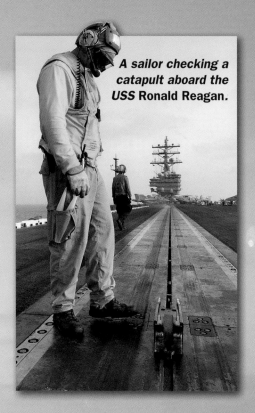

A sailor checking a catapult aboard the USS Ronald Reagan.

XTREME FACT

Using a catapult, a 60,000-pound (27,216-kg) aircraft can reach 150 miles per hour (241 kph) in less than two seconds.

LANDING

Planes land in the flight deck's recovery area. It is angled so that planes can take off and land at the same time without colliding.

When an aircraft lands, its tailhook snags a steel cable running across the flight deck. These arresting cables bring the plane to a complete stop. Flight crews then quickly move the aircraft aside to make room for other planes to land.

Pilots use a device called an Optical Landing System, nicknamed the "meatball." It has colored lights that warn if a plane is too high or low to safely land.

Aircraft Carrier Flight Deck

Elevator Arresting Meatball Catapults
Cables

Elevator   The Island   Elevators   Catapults

GLOSSARY

CAPITAL SHIP
A capital ship is a navy's most powerful and most important warship. Before the age of flight, battleships were usually capital ships. Today, aircraft carriers play the leading role in the fleets of many navies. The United States Navy has 11 capital ships. All are aircraft carriers.

DISPLACEMENT
Displacement is a way of measuring a ship's mass, or size. It equals the weight of the water a ship displaces, or occupies, while floating. Think of a bathtub filled to the rim with water. A toy boat placed in the tub would cause water to spill over the sides. The weight of that water equals the weight of the boat.

HULL
The hull is the main body of a ship. It includes the bottom, sides and deck.

MEATBALL
If it very difficult to land on an aircraft carrier. The ship is moving on the ocean, the weather can be unpredictable, and sometimes a landing has to happen

at night. During the approach, it is hard for a pilot to know if the plane is too high or too low to land safely. Too high, and the plane will overshoot the runway. Too low, and it will crash into the back of the ship. Landing Signal Officers give a pilot instructions by radio. In addition, a series of lights called the Optical Landing System are installed on the flight deck. The center light, nicknamed the meatball, is an amber light between a row of green horizontal lights. If all the lights are aligned, the pilot knows the plane is on the proper glide path and can be landed safely.

RADAR

A way to detect objects, such as aircraft or ships, using electromagnetic (radio) waves. Radar waves are sent out by large dishes, or antennas, and then strike an object. The radar dish then detects the reflected wave, which can tell operators how big an object is, how fast it is moving, its altitude, and its direction.

TAILHOOK

A tailhook is a strong metal hook attached to a plane's tail that extends downward. When landing on an aircraft carrier, a pilot tries to snag the tailhook on one of four arresting cables that are strung across the deck. When a cable is snagged, it stretches out, and a hydraulic cylinder system absorbs the plane's energy, bringing it to a quick stop on the flight deck.

INDEX